T0358161

I LOVE MY DOG
AND MY DOG LOVES ME

I LOVE MY DOG
AND MY DOG LOVES ME

Gillie and Marc Schattner

Wakefield
Press

Wakefield Press
1 The Parade West
Kent Town
South Australia 5067
www.wakefieldpress.com.au

First published 2009
Copyright © Gillie and Marc Schattner, 2009

National Library of Australia Cataloguing-in-Publication entry

Title:	I love my dog and my dog loves me/
	illustrators, Gillie Schattner, Marc Schattner.
ISBN:	978 1 86254 837 4 (hbk.).
Subjects:	Dogs – Pictorial works.
Other Authors/Contributors:	Schattner, Gillie.
	Schattner, Marc.
Dewey Number:	758.3

Paintings and book design by Gillie and Marc Schattner
The paintings are acrylic on canvas
Printed in China at Everbest Printing Co. Ltd

Have you ever known a dog who doesn't love his owner?

My dog throws me a welcome home party every time I walk in the door. He accompanies me through life-changing experiences, loves me no matter what, never gets moody, and is always fun to have around, even if it's a dog of a day.

Dogs represent everything that's best in us.

This book is dedicated to Moby,
the devoted friend who is always by our side.

I LOVE MY DOG,
AND HE LOVES ME,
BECAUSE ...

HE LOVES THE THRILL
OF THE CHASE

HE DOESN'T OVER-ANALYZE

GILLIE AND MARC

HE LOVES A GOOD FEED

GILLIE AND MARC

I AM THE NICEST PERSON
HE HAS EVER MET

AND THE SMARTEST

GILLIE AND MARC

AND THE WITTIEST

GILLIE AND MARC

HE LIVES IN THE MOMENT

HE ALWAYS THINKS THE BEST
OF ME EVEN WHEN
I DON'T DESERVE IT

GILLIE AND MARC

HE ADMIRES ME AS
IF I WERE NAPOLEON

GILLIE AND MARC

HE UNDERSTANDS THE
SPECIAL GENIUS
OF MY CONVERSATION

GILLIE AND MARC

MY SKILLS AND TALENTS
ARE AWE-INSPIRING

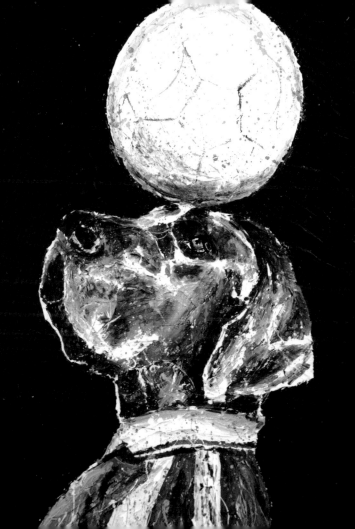

GILLIE AND MARC

HE KNOWS SOME THINGS
SHOULD BE SAVOURED

THIS IS OUR MOMENT
IN THE SUN

GILLIE AND MARC

HE'S A PARTY ANIMAL

GILLIE AND MARC

HE'S AT ONE WITH
THE UNIVERSE

CILLIE AND MARC

HE'S ALWAYS ENTERTAINING

HE'D SACRIFICE HIS
LIFE FOR MINE

HE GETS IT,
EVEN WHEN HE DOESN'T

GILLIE AND MARC

MY LOVE DOES NOT
EMBARRASS HIM

GILLIE AND MARC

JUST BECAUSE

GILLIE AND MARC

Gillie and Marc Schattner
are best selling authors and illustrators of
The Happiest Day of My Life,
The Perfect Gift,
and *True Love*.

As artists their work has been shown in solo exhibitions in Sydney, New York, Singapore, Hong Kong and Belgium. Their work has also appeared in group shows all over the world.

Gillie and Marc work collaboratively, so that every artwork, from paintings to books to sculpture, is a joint creation. In 2006 they were finalists in the Archibald Portrait Prize.

They live in Sydney with their two children, Jessie and Ben, a cat, and a dog.

More information can be found at **www.gillieandmarc.com**

Special thanks to:

Bryce Courtenay
Christine Gee
Mardi McConnochie

Richard Martin
Linton and Kay
Libby Edwards Galleries

Jessica Schattner
Ben Schattner